Novels for Students, Volume 44

Project Editor: Sara Constantakis Rights Acquisition and Management: Sheila Spencer Composition: Evi Abou-El-Seoud Manufacturing: Rhonda Dover

Imaging: John Watkins

Product Design: Pamela A. E. Galbreath, Jennifer Wahi Digital Content Production: Allie Semperger Product Manager: Meggin Condino © 2014 Gale, Cengage Learning

For product information and technology assistance, contact us at
Gale Customer Support, 1-800-877-4253.
For permission to use material from this text or product,
submit all requests online at
www.cengage.com/permissions.
Further permissions questions can be emailed to
permissionrequest@cengage.com While every effort has been made to ensure the reliability of the information presented in this publication, Gale, a part of Cengage Learning, does not guarantee the accuracy of the data contained herein. Gale accepts no payment for listing; and inclusion in the publication of any organization, agency, institution, publication, service, or individual does not imply endorsement of the editors or publisher. Errors brought to the attention of the publisher and verified to the satisfaction of the publisher will be corrected in future editions.

Gale
27500 Drake Rd.
Farmington Hills, MI, 48331-3535

ISBN-13: 978-1-4144-9487-6
ISBN-10: 1-4144-9487-4
ISSN 1094-3552

This title is also available as an e-book.
ISBN-13: 978-1-4144-9273-5
ISBN-10: 1-4144-9273-1
Contact your Gale, a part of Cengage Learning sales
representative for ordering information.

Printed in Mexico
1 2 3 4 5 6 7 17 16 15 14 13

The Book Thief

MARKUS ZUSAK

2005

INTRODUCTION

Markus Zusak's novel *The Book Thief* features a unique narrator telling the tale of Liesel Meminger, a young German girl who finds her life during World War II increasingly tied to books—many of which, as the title suggests, are stolen. Seemingly abandoned by her parents and witness to her younger brother's death by illness, Liesel is sent to live with a foster family in a small town outside Munich. There, she begins a relationship with books that challenges and sustains her during the darkest moments of war—and, ultimately, even saves her life.

Zusak was already a successful children's book author before *The Book Thief*, with four previously published novels. One of these, *I Am the Messenger* (originally published in Australia as *The Messenger*, 2002), was even chosen as Book of the Year by the Children's Book Council of Australia. However, *The Book Thief* was a special work for the author: The youngest child of German and Austrian parents who later settled in Australia, Zusak grew up hearing tales of wartime Germany. He wanted to show readers that not all Germans were hateful and brutal. As Zusak states in an interview featured in the reader's guide of the paperback edition of the novel, "I wanted them to see people who were unwilling to fly the Nazi flag, and boys and girls who thought the Hitler Youth was boring and ridiculous."

Published first in Australia in 2005, *The Book Thief* became one of the most popular works of young-adult fiction of 2006 internationally, topping the *New York Times* children's best-seller list and enjoying significant readership among adults as well. The book was Zusak's second named a Michael L. Printz Honor Book; more importantly, it has sparked the imaginations of readers around the world with its resonant message about the power of words. As Zusak himself puts it,

> I thought of Hitler destroying people with words, and now I had a girl who was stealing them back. ... She writes her own story—and it's a

beautiful story—through the ugliness
of the world that surrounds her.

AUTHOR BIOGRAPHY

Markus Zusak was born on June 23, 1975, and raised in Sydney, Australia. He is the youngest child of a German mother and an Austrian father. Growing up, he heard many tales about life and the times in Germany during World War II. Some of these events, such as the Allied bombing of Munich and the marching of Jews through towns to nearby concentration camps, would serve as key elements in *The Book Thief*.

Zusak's first novel was *The Underdog*, published in Australia in 1999. The book concerns a teenager named Cameron Wolfe and his struggles to become a man in his working-class Australian neighborhood. Two more novels followed, *Fighting Ruben Wolfe and When Dogs Cry* (published in the United States as *Getting the Girl*), also about Cameron and the Wolfe clan. *When Dogs Cry* was selected as an Honor Book by the Children's Book Council of Australia. Zusak's follow-up, *The Messenger* (2002; US release as *I Am the Messenger* in 2005), earned Zusak further acclaim. The novel was named a Michael L. Printz Honor Book, a young-adult commendation given by the American Library Association, and was nominated for the *Los Angeles Times* Book Prize.

Zusak's most successful work to date is *The Book Thief*, which has topped the best-seller lists in several countries and became the author's second

Michael L. Printz Honor Book. The novel won the 2006 National Jewish Book Award for Children's and Young Adults' Literature. As of 2012, Zusak was living with his wife and children in his native Sydney, where he occasionally works as an English teacher and continues to write.

Prologue: A Mountain Range of Rubble

The Book Thief begins with an introduction by its narrator, Death. He offers a brief explanation for his involvement in the story about to begin. As Death, he explains, he occupies himself by taking note of the color of the sky at the moment he takes the soul of a dying person. This is also, he points out, a way to keep from noticing the living—the survivors "who are left behind, crumbling among the jigsaw puzzle of realization, despair, and surprise." Sometimes, however, a survivor catches his eye during the course of his work; one of these is a girl he calls "the book thief," whom he has seen three times while taking the souls of others.

The first time he saw the girl he was outside a train in the snow, under a blinding white sky.

The girl's young brother had suddenly died as the two journeyed by train with their mother. The second time was years later, when the girl appeared at the site of a crashed plane under a black sky; the pilot was not yet dead when she arrived. The third time was under a glowing red sky, among the ruins of a devastated city. The girl, standing dazed in the bombed-out remains of her former neighborhood, dropped the book she was holding. Death watched as workers piled the book onto a stack of garbage to be hauled away, and on an impulse he acted: "I climbed aboard and took it in my hand, not realizing that I would keep it and view it several thousand times over the years." The story that follows is the tale of the book thief and her experiences between Death's first and third encounter with her.

Part One: The Grave Digger's Handbook

In January 1939, the book thief—whose name is Liesel Meminger—is only nine years old. She and her brother are being taken by their mother to Munich, where they are to be taken in by foster parents with the hope of receiving a better life. Their father is absent, and though Liesel does not understand why, she draws a connection between him and the word "Communist," which she hears in hushed adult conversations. Riding on the train toward Munich, Liesel wakes from a nap and notices that her brother Werner has died.

Liesel and her mother bury Werner at the next town. While at the cemetery, Liesel—who has trouble understanding the loss of her brother—stumbles upon a small black book that has been dropped in the snow. She takes it.

Outside Munich, in the small town of Molching, Liesel is left with a woman who drives her to her new home. Her foster parents are Rosa and Hans Hubermann, a middle-aged couple who live on Himmel Street in an impoverished section of town. Their own two children are grown and living away from home. Hans is a soft-spoken man whose eyes are "made of kindness, and silver," while Rosa is a plump, abrasive woman who refers to most people as filthy pigs—in German, *Saukerl* (for males) or *Saumensch* (for females). Hans is a painter by trade, though he also loves playing the accordion and rolling his own cigarettes. Rosa washes laundry for some of the wealthier Molching families—including Mayor Hermann and his wife— as a way of bringing in some much-needed money.

Liesel is enrolled in both school and the BDM, a Hitler Youth group for young girls. Though she has already taken a book—which she keeps under her mattress—Liesel cannot read or write when she begins school. She is also haunted nightly by nightmares about her brother's death. Both problems are dealt with by Hans, who sits with Liesel each night when she wakes in terror; eventually they begin late-night readings of the book she took from the cemetery, which she discovers is called *The Grave Digger's Handbook*. Hans begins teaching her to write on the only paper in the house: the backsides of sandpaper sheets he uses when painting. When the sandpaper runs out, they begin painting words on the walls of the basement.

Liesel makes a few friends at school, most notably Rudy Steiner, a boy known throughout the neighborhood for blackening himself with charcoal and impersonating Jesse Owens three years prior. She also has one notable enemy, however, at least for a time: Ludwig Schmeikl, a boy who takes pleasure in ridiculing Liesel's still-faltering skills at reading. Liesl is already upset and humiliated. Ludwig's words break her confidence, and she beats him up during recess.

MEDIA ADAPTATIONS

- An unabridged audio recording of *The Book Thief* was released by Listening Library in 2006. The book is read by Allan Corduner and is available on compact disc or as an audio download through Amazon.com.

- An e-book version of *The Book Thief* was released by Knopf Books for Young Readers in the Kindle format in 2007, available online at Amazon.com.

Part Two: The Shoulder Shrug

By the close of 1939, Liesel has finished reading *The Grave Digger's Handbook* with Hans and has adjusted well to her new life in Molching. For Christmas, she receives two books from her foster father; she discovers that he traded away much of his treasured tobacco ration in order to buy them.

The following month, Liesel and her classmates are tasked with writing a letter. She chooses to write to her biological mother and sends it through the foster-care agency, hoping that somehow the letter will find her mother and bring a response. She watches the mail each day for three months, even after foster-care agents admit to not knowing the mother's location. Liesel even mails off additional letters by taking portions of Rosa's ever-dwindling laundry earnings in order to buy stamps. She is discovered, and starts to receive a beating; when Rosa finds out the reason for the thievery, however, she apologizes. Liesel comes to the realization that "she would never see her mother again."

In April 1940, the entire town of Molching prepares to celebrate Hitler's birthday with a bonfire. The adult Hubermann children, Hans Junior and Trudy, also return home for the event. Hans Junior, a zealous member of the Nazi Party, butts heads with his more moderate father, who has yet to be accepted as a member of the party but does not seem to mind. Trudy works as a housemaid in

Munich, and Liesel finds her quiet but pleasant. During an argument, Hans Junior calls his father a coward and storms out of the house. Death hints at his future fate: "Yes, the boy was gone, and I wish I could tell you that everything worked out for the younger Hans Hubermann, but it didn't."

Liesel leaves the house to attend the bonfire as part of her Hitler Youth group. She is stunned when she discovers that the fuel for the bonfire is a mountain of books. She is further taken aback when the Nazi speaker rattles off a list of enemies to Germany—including "communists," a word somehow connected to her father. She struggles to escape through the crowd and finds an unlikely ally among the press of people: Ludwig Schmeikl, the boy she had beaten up for teasing her. His ankle has been injured during the chaos, and she helps him to safety. The two apologize for their past behaviors to each other.

Later, Liesel meets her foster father by the smoking remains of the bonfire. She asks him if her mother was a Communist, and if Hitler took her away. He answers honestly: "I think he might have, yes." When she tells him that she hates Hitler, he slaps her and warns her never to say such a thing in public again. It is an uncharacteristic act for the normally gentle man, which drives home the importance of the message. While her foster father speaks with an acquaintance, Liesel watches as workers dampen the embers and shovel away the burned remains of the bonfire. Near the bottom of the heap, she sees three books that have escaped the flames. When no one is looking, she reaches in and pulls out the closest of the books. She shoves it into her jacket, though it is still hot and smoking. Only afterward does she realize that someone has seen her thievery—the mayor's wife, Ilsa Hermann.

Part Three: Mein Kampf

On the way home from the bonfire, Hans discovers Liesel's secret theft. Rather than becoming upset, it seems to spark an idea in him. He later walks to the local Nazi Party office and trades some money and cigarettes for a used copy of Hitler's autobiography, *Mein Kampf*.

Soon after, Liesel visits the mayor's house to drop off laundry for her mother. She is relieved when the mayor's wife makes no mention of the book-stealing incident. The next time she visits, Ilsa Hermann beckons Liesel inside. The woman shows the girl a wondrous sight: an entire room with each wall filled to the ceiling with books. Thereafter, every time she stops at the mayor's house for laundry delivery or pickup, she spends time reading books in the library while Ilsa looks on. Liesel discovers that the Hermanns had once had a son, but he died during World War I. Ilsa Hermann is certain that he froze to death, and in a sort of punishment to herself, she always leaves the window to the library open—even in the dead of winter.

Hans sends the used copy of *Mein Kampf* to a Jew in hiding named Max Vandenburg, along with a key taped inside the cover. Hans knows that any other shipment might be suspect, but a copy of *Mein Kampf* is likely to pass unnoticed by an official searching through parcels; it would also divert suspicion from a Jew if he were to be seen reading the book in public. Max leaves his hiding place in Stuttgart and, using fake identification, boards a train headed toward Molching. He walks the last portion of the journey and arrives at the Hubermann household at night. He uses the key from the book to let himself in.

Part Four: The Standover Man

Hans Hubermann's connection to Max Vandenburg is revealed: Hans Hubermann fought during World War I with Max's father, Erik. Indeed, Erik was the one who taught Hans how to play the accordion. One day, just before their company entered combat, the sergeant asked for a volunteer with good penmanship. Knowing that the volunteer would avoid combat and have the best chance at surviving the day, Erik recommended his friend Hans for the job. In doing so, he saved Hans's life and lost his own. Hans was later given the only possession of Erik's that was too big to send home to his family: his accordion. After the war, Hans visited Erik's widow in Stuttgart; to his surprise, he discovered that Erik had a son. Hans left the woman his name and address in Molching and told her to contact him if she ever needed a favor, such as painting her apartment—his only skill.

The root of Hans's uneasy relationship with the

Nazi Party is also revealed: as a painter, he became infamous for helping Jews whose homes and businesses had been painted over with slurs and insults. Also, although he had applied to be a member of the party in 1937, he made a clumsy and aborted attempt to withdraw his application after seeing some vandals throwing bricks through the window of a Jewish businessman's shop. Thereafter, he was regarded with suspicion.

Hans also reveals how Max came to their home. Hans was visited in June 1939 by a man named Walter Kugler from Stuttgart. Walter was a longtime friend—and frequent fist-fighting opponent—of Max Vandenburg. Walter had been hiding Max for two years but was fearful that he would be discovered. Walter found Hans thanks to the scrap of paper he had left with Max's mother twenty years before; seeing it as a way to repay his long-dead friend, Hans agreed to help Max.

Oncein the Hubermann house, Maxsleeps for three days straight. When Max wakes, Liesel's is the first face he sees. Hans explains the situation to Liesel, makingclear that the presence of Maxmust never berevealed to anyone. Foreveryone's safety, Hans fashions a small, secret living space under the basement stairs for Max; when winter arrives, however, Max is allowed upstairs at night to sleep near the fire. In February, when she turns twelve, Liesel receives a book titled *The Mud Men*. Max, unable to give her anything, comes up with an idea: he removes some of the pages from the copy of *Mein Kampf* that Hans sent him, paints over the words, and writes his own story—featuring himself, Liesel, and crude illustrations—called "The Standover Man." She treasures it.

Part Five: The Whistler

Throughout the spring of 1941, Liesel continues her visits to Ilsa Hermann's library every time she stops by for laundry pickup. She becomes hooked on a book called *The Whistler*, about a murderer who whistled as he fled the scenes of his crimes. She also strengthens her bond with Max; she brings him discarded newspapers so he can do the crosswords, and she tells him what the weather is like since he cannot venture outdoors himself. The whole family also helps Max paint over the remaining pages of *Mein Kampf* so he can continue his writings and sketches.

In June, as the war intensifies in places far from Molching, Ilsa Hermann hands Liesel a letter terminating her foster mother's employment—and with it, the last trace of Rosa Hubermann's meager income. Ilsa also insists that Liesel take *The Whistler* as a gift. She does, but later returns to give back the book and unload a torrent of anger and insults at the wealthy woman.

Meanwhile, Rudy Steiner endures frequent abuse at the hands of his Hitler Youth leader, Franz Deutscher. One day, after being humiliated by Deutscher, Rudy asks Liesel to go steal something with him to improve his mood. Liesel takes him to the mayor's house, knowing that Ilsa Hermann leaves the window open in the library. Instead of stealing food like Rudy wants, she sneaks in and steals *The Whistler*. Rudy stops attending Hitler Youth in order to avoid Deutscher; eventually, thanks to his brother Kurt, Rudy is reassigned to a different Hitler Youth group.

Part Six: *The Dream Carrier*

Shortly after Christmas 1942—an event highlighted by Liesel, her foster parents, and Max building a snowman in the basement using buckets of snow from outside their house—Max's health begins to decline. In February, he collapses and falls unconscious. The Hubermanns place him upstairs in Liesel's bed to recover. Liesel gathers discarded items from the outside world and leaves them next to him as gifts, somehow believing they might help him get better and wake up. She also reads to him each day, and even makes a trip with Rudy to the mayor's house to steal another book for Max to listen to; the book is called *The Dream Carrier*.

Max remains unconscious for over a month, and the Hubermanns begin to fear that he will die—leaving them not only with grief, but also with the additional danger of having a dead Jew in their house. Finally, one day while Liesel is at school, Rosa visits on the pretense of yelling at the girl for stealing her hair brush; the real message, however—whispered under her breath—is that Max is finally awake. By April, he has fully recovered and reclaimed his living space in the basement.

In June, however, members of the Nazi Party make the rounds throughout the neighborhood, inspecting basements to determine which are the deepest—and therefore most suitable to serve as bomb shelters in the event of an Allied attack. Liesel notices the inspectors and acts quickly to warn her family. They contemplate moving Max out of the basement, but Hans decides it would be best to leave him hidden there behind the drop sheets and paint cans that cover his living space. The Nazi inspector spends three long minutes in the basement, to then inform Hans that it is too shallow to serve as a bomb shelter. Max has gone undiscovered, and they all narrowly escape an awful fate.

Part Seven: The Complete Duden Dictionary and Thesaurus

As the citizens of Molching prepare for possible attack, Hans Hubermann enjoys a resurgence in his painting business, blackening windows to make internal lights invisible to nighttime bombers. Liesel often goes with her father to help him paint and loves hearing him tell stories of his life.

Throughout the summer, Rudy practices his running in preparation for a competition at a Hitler Youth carnival. Rudy wins three of the four race events, relishing his victories over Franz Deutscher. In his final event, however, he is disqualified for jumping the starting gun. Rudy later confesses that he did it on purpose, though he does not explain himself.

Liesel steals another book from the library of the mayor's house, titled *A Song in the Dark*. Soon after, Rudy shows Liesel something unusual: at the mayor's house, the window to the library is closed, but a book rests against it on the inside. Liesel lifts the window and takes it. *The book is The Complete Duden Dictionary and Thesaurus*, and inside is a letter for Liesel from Ilsa Hermann. Ilsa informs Liesel that she knows the girl has been entering the library and stealing books, but she does not mind. She writes, "My only hope is that one day you will knock on the front door and enter the library in the more civilized manner."

One September night, the Hubermann household wakes to the sirens warning of a coming air raid. They hurry to the nearest approved shelter, the basement of a family named the Fiedlers. Other occupants include Rudy and his family and Frau Holtzapfel—a spiteful neighbor engaged in a long-standing feud with Rosa Hubermann. This first warning, they later discover, was a false alarm. It is soon followed, however, by another real warning. Crowded in a basement filled with fearful civilians, Liesel opens *The Whistler* and begins reading in an attempt to calm everyone down. Soon enough, they are all engrossed in the tale; when the siren sounds to indicate safety, they all remain in place to allow Liesel to finish reading the first chapter. They return home to find that Molching has narrowly escaped the bombs.

In the days that follow, Frau Holtzapfel appears at the Hubermanns' front door. She tells Liesel that she enjoyed the first chapter of *The Whistler* and would like the girl to come to her house regularly and read her the rest of the book. In exchange, Frau Holtzapfel agrees to stop spitting on the Hubermanns' front door—a nasty tradition spawned from her feud with Rosa—and also agrees to give the Hubermanns her ration of coffee.

Soon after, a group of Nazi soldiers decides to march their cargo of Jews through the streets of Molching on their way to the concentration camp at Dachau. As the residents watch, one of the Jews falls behind and repeatedly drops to his knees, only to be forced back to his feet by the soldiers. As he passes, Hans Hubermann walks out into the assembly of Jews and gives the man a piece of bread. Both the Jew and Hans receive lashes from a whip; Hans's paint cart is overturned, and he is called a Jew lover.

Only afterward does Hans realize that his actions have placed his family and Max in jeopardy. Fearing that Nazi officials will come to search their house, Max packs his things and departs under cover of night. He tells Liesel that he has left her something but that she will not receive it until the time is right.

Part Eight: The Word Shaker

Despite Hans Hubermann's fears, Nazi officials come not for him but for Rudy Steiner. His excellent academic and athletic abilities have attracted their attention, and they would like the boy to attend a special school. His fearful father, however, refuses to let him go.

In November, Hans Hubermann is surprised to finally receive a letter approving his application to be a member of the Nazi Party. It is followed soon after by a draft notice enlisting him to serve in the German army. Liesel soon discovers that Rudy's father, Alex, will suffer the same fate. One night, after Hans has left for the war, Liesel wakes to find Rosa—usually so loud and often outwardly callous —sitting on her bed, silently holding her husband's accordion.

Instead of being sent to Russia as he fears, Hans remains in Germany as part of a unit of soldiers known among themselves as "Dead Body Collectors," tasked with cleaning up the devastation caused by Allied air raids. Alex serves in Vienna, using his skills as a tailor to repair clothing destined for soldiers fighting in Russia.

In December 1942, another parade of Jews is marched through Molching. Rudy decides to leave bread in the street for the hungry Jews to take— inspired by Hans Hubermann's infamous act of generosity—and Liesel helps him. They are chased off by Nazi soldiers, but only after some of the Jews find and eat the offerings. Liesel is both disappointed and gladdened that Max is not among the captured Jews. For Christmas, Rosa gives Liesel a final gift from Max, which she had been holding onto at his request. It is another book created by him, titled *The Word Shaker*. It is a dreamlike tale of a girl, the power of words, and the young man who inspires her to use them.

Part Nine: The Last Human Stranger

Liesel returns to the mayor's house and takes another book, *The Last Human Stranger*, along with a plate of cookies that has been left for her. She is surprised when Ilsa Hermann opens the door and finds her there; they have a brief but pleasant conversation. Later, Liesel meets Frau Holtzapfel's son Michael, who lost a hand fighting in Stalingrad; her other son, Robert, died there. Michael informs Rosa that Hans Junior is fighting there as well, but his fate is unknown.

Hans, while preparing to ride out with his unit for clean-up duty, is forced to switch seats with an intimidating soldier named Reinhold Zucker. The truck they ride in blows a tire and loses control, flipping several times. Hans suffers a broken leg, but Zucker—having taken Hans's usual seat—is killed. Because of his injury, Hans is sent back home.

Part Ten: The Book Thief

In July 1943, a few months after Hans has returned home, Michael Holtzapfel hangs himself, guilt-ridden over the loss of his brother. In August, Liesel—who makes a habit of searching the occasional parades of captured Jews—finds Max Vandenburg. She runs to Max and embraces him, undeterred by the cracking whips of the Nazi overseers. The soldiers separate them, and Rudy holds Liesel back as Max is taken away. She later reveals the secret of Max's hiding to Rudy.

Liesel sneaks once more into Ilsa Hermann's library for another book, but she becomes angry over the unfairness of the world and instead tears a book apart. She leaves a letter of apology and promises never to return. Three days later, Ilsa Hermann visits her at home. She brings a special book as a gift: a book of empty pages. She tells the girl, "I thought if you're not going to read any more of my books, you might like to write one instead." Liesel takes her advice, and working in the basement that once housed a hidden Jew, she begins writing a memoir of her life from the time her young brother died. She calls it *The Book Thief*. She finishes the book in October with the following line: "I have hated the words and I have loved them, and I hope I have made them right."

Five nights later, while Liesel is in the basement rereading her book, the bombs finally fall on Molching without warning, as the city sleeps. Everyone on her street is killed—Hans and Rosa Hubermann, Frau Holtzapfel, Rudy Steiner and his siblings—except Liesel, who happened to be in the safest place possible. She is buried beneath the rubble, but when workers find her, she is unhurt. Dazed and unable to comprehend the devastation, she drops her book and cries out for her papa, Hans.

Epilogue: The Last Color

Death does not encounter Liesel Meminger for many years after that. In fact, he states, "I should tell you that the book thief died only yesterday." When Death finally visits Liesel as an old woman in Sydney, Australia, he is able to glimpse additional details of her life after the bombing through fragments of her memories. After her street was destroyed, Liesel was taken in by Ilsa Hermann and her husband, the mayor. Erik Steiner returned from the war to find that his family had been killed; eventually he reopened his clothing shop, and Liesel often worked there with him. In October 1945, after the end of the war, Liesel was reunited with Max Vandenburg, who was fortunate enough to survive the concentration camps.

Conversing with Death, Liesel is surprised that he has kept and read her book so many times. She wants to know if it is possible for Death to understand a story so centered on life and living. Death simply responds, "I am haunted by humans."

CHARACTERS

Arthur Berg

Arthur Berg is the leader of a group of youngsters who steal various things in and around Molching. Rudy and Liesel briefly join his gang of thieves, stealing items such as potatoes and onions. He is a generous leader, sharing his various takes with Liesel and Rudy. Arthur later moves to Cologne, where his younger sister is killed—presumably by Allied bombing.

Herbert Bollinger

Herbert Bollinger is an old acquaintance of Hans Hubermann's. When Hans notices in the mid-1930s that the number of customers for his painting business are dwindling, Bollinger points out that he should be a member of the Nazi Party if he wants to keep working.

Viktor Chemmel

Viktor Chemmel is the young man who takes over as leader of the gang of young thieves previously led by Arthur Berg. After Viktor offers Liesel and Rudy almost nothing for their efforts on a thievery run, Rudy insults him, and Viktor beats him up. Later, Viktor throws one of Liesel's books into the river.

Death

Death is the narrator of *The Book Thief* and participates in the story by taking the lives of many of the characters at various times. He first notices Liesel when he takes the life of her young brother, Werner. Later, after he collects the many victims of the bombing on Himmel Street, he finds Liesel's memoir on a pile of trash and takes it. From it he learns Liesel's story, which he shares with the reader.

Franz Deutscher

Franz Deutscher is Rudy Steiner and Tommy Müller's sadistic Hitler Youth leader. When Tommy fails to hear his commands during marching, both Tommy and Rudy—who stands up for his friend—become his favorite targets of punishment. After Rudy moves to a different Hitler Youth group, he takes pleasure in winning several events at an athletic competition as Deutscher looks on.

Frau Diller

Frau Diller is the owner of the corner shop on Himmel Street. An avid supporter of the Nazi Party, she demands that everyone offer a salutary "*heil* Hitler" when they enter her store.

The Fiedlers

The Fiedlers are the family with the deepest basement on Himmel Street, which is thus chosen as the meeting location for Himmel Street residents in the event of an air raid. It is in their basement that Liesel calms both the children and adults by reading excerpts from *The Whistler*. Like the others on Himmel Street, they die during a surprise bombing by Allied planes.

Rolf Fischer

Rolf Fischer is a leading member of the Nazi Party in Molching. In 1937, he sees Hans Hubermann painting over the door of Joel Kleinmann, a Jewish store owner, after it had been marked by a Star of David and the words "Jewish filth." This is part of the reason why Hans Hubermann is not accepted as a member of the Nazi Party until many years later.

Frau Heinrich

Frau Heinrich is the foster-care agent who transports Liesel on her final journey to her new home with the Hubermanns. When Liesel arrives, she is at first unwilling to get out of Frau Heinrich's car. Later, when Hans Hubermann contacts her regarding the whereabouts of Liesel's biological mother, she states that she does not know where the woman is.

Heinz Hermann

Heinz Hermann is the mayor of Molching and husband of Ilsa Hermann. In June 1941, he mentions in an interview for the local paper that the citizens of Molching should prepare for harder times to come. A week later, he and his wife fire Rosa Hubermann as their launderer. After the bombing of Himmel Street, Heinz and Ilsa take Liesel in and raise her as their own.

Ilsa Hermann

Ilsa Hermann is the wife of the mayor of Molching, Heinz Hermann. Liesel's foster mother, Rosa, washes their laundry, and the Hermanns are her last remaining customers until they, too, must stop using her services as the war rages on. On the day of the bonfire, she sees Liesel steal a book from the charred remains; she later invites Liesel to use her library, which Liesel does on a regular basis, forging a bond between the two. After Himmel Street is destroyed, Ilsa and Heinz Hermann take Liesel in as their own.

Frau Holtzapfel

Frau Holtzapfel is the next-door neighbor of the Hubermanns. She and Rosa Hubermann are longtime enemies for an unknown reason, and Frau Holtzapfel faithfully spits on the Hubermann's front door every time she passes. After being huddled together in a basement during an air raid, Frau

Holtzapfel makes a deal with Rosa: she will stop spitting on her door if Liesel will visit her regularly and read to her from one of her books.

Michael Holtzapfel

Michael Holtzapfel is one of Frau Holtzapfel's two sons. He loses his hand fighting in Stalingrad, while his brother dies there. After he returns home to live with Frau Holtzapfel, he cannot overcome the guilt of surviving when his brother did not. He eventually commits suicide by hanging himself.

Hans Hubermann

Hans Hubermann is Liesel's foster father, her reading teacher, and eventually the most significant person in her life. He is a tall, quiet man with a gentle nature whose sympathy for Jews results in his being eyed with suspicion by local members of the Nazi Party, as well as by his son, Hans Junior. He agrees to secretly harbor a Jew named Max Vandenburg in his basement, an arrangement that places him and his family in great danger. Although he escapes death twice as a soldier, he is killed during the Allied bombing of Himmel Street.

Hans Hubermann Junior

Hans Hubermann Junior is the adult son of Hans and Rosa Hubermann. A faithful member of the Nazi Party, he has arguments with his father over the older man's apparent lack of support for

Nazism. After one argument, on the day of Hitler's birthday celebration, Hans Junior leaves his parents' house and never returns. He later dies in combat in Russia.

Rosa Hubermann

Rosa Hubermann is Liesel's foster mother and lives on Himmel Street in the small town of Molching with her husband, Hans. She is a brash, strict woman who frequently refers to those around her as filthy pigs. Later, Liesel realizes that Rosa's harsh exterior masks a deep love for the people in her life. Like most of the residents of Himmel Street, she is killed by Allied bombs during an air strike.

Trudy Hubermann

Trudy is the adult daughter of Hans and Rosa Hubermann. She works as a housemaid for a family in Munich and occasionally returns to Molching on holidays to visit her parents. She is quiet but kind, like her father.

Joel Kleinmann

Joel Kleinmann is the Jewish owner of a shoe store in Molching. When his shop is vandalized in 1937, Hans Hubermann paints over a slur that has been written on his door.

Walter Kugler

Walter Kugler is a childhood friend of Max Vandenburg's. The two often fist-fought each other as part of a friendly rivalry. When Max faces persecution and possible imprisonment as a Jew, Kugler—who is not a Jew and therefore safe from the reach of Nazis—hides Max for nearly two years. When Kugler finds out he is being relocated to Poland, he meets with Hans Hubermann to see if Hans will help Max hide.

Liesel Meminger

Liesel Meminger, the main character in *The Book Thief*, is a girl who is left in the care of a foster family at a young age. Her brother dies on the way to the foster home, and at the cemetery where he is buried, Liesel sees a book resting in the snow. She takes it, and thus begins her career as a book thief. Ilsa Hermann catches her stealing a book and invites her to borrow more books from her massive library. Liesel becomes an avid reader, and Ilsa Hermann eventually encourages her to write her own book. She does, working in the basement of her foster family's home, where she once spent time with Max Vandenburg, a Jew in hiding. One night, while Liesel is reading over her finished book in the basement, Allied forces bomb Himmel Street, killing everyone except for Liesel. She is then taken in and raised by Ilsa Hermann and her husband, the mayor. The book she has written, lost in the rubble of Himmel Street, is found by Death and kept as an example of how humans are as capable of wonderful things as they are of horrible things.

Paula Meminger

Liesel's biological mother, Paula Meminger, leaves Liesel with a foster family in Munich and, though Liesel later tries to contact her, disappears. Liesel later figures out that it is likely she was taken away by Hitler for being a Communist.

Werner Meminger

Werner Meminger, Liesel's younger brother, dies after having a coughing fit on the train journey to Munich with his mother and sister. Liesel and her mother bury the boy at a local cemetery before continuing their journey; this cemetery is where Liesel steals her first book, *The Grave Digger's Handbook*.

Tommy Müller

Tommy Müller is a boy who lives on Himmel Street and goes to school with Liesel and Rudy. Plagued by chronic ear infections and scarred by several related operations, Tommy is partially deaf and prone to facial twitches. Rudy Steiner stands up for Tommy during Nazi Youth activities after he fails to hear commands, and both boys are frequently punished together. Like the others on Himmel Street, he is killed during the Allied bombing.

Pfiffikus

Pfiffikus is a foul-mouthed old man who lives on Himmel Street. No one seems to know his real name, but he is called Pfiffikus because he constantly whistles a tune as he walks. He is one of the Himmel Street residents who later shares the Fiedlers' basement during air raids.

Boris Schipper

Sergeant Boris Schipper is Hans Hubermann's commanding officer when he is called to serve as a clean-up soldier during World War II. After Hans is injured when their transport truck rolls over, Schipper—who likes Hans due to his generosity when he wins at cards—recommends that Hans be allowed to return home and work in an office in Munich.

Ludwig Schmeikl

Ludwig Schmeikl is a boy in Liesel's class who teases her for being unable to read during her first months in Molching. One day during recess, after he relentlessly insults her, Liesel snaps and gives him a serious beating. The two later make amends during the bonfire at Hitler's birthday celebration.

Stephan Schneider

Stephan Schneider is the officer in charge of Hans Hubermann and Erik Vandenburg's unit during their service in World War I. One day, he offers one soldier a chance to perform a noncombat-related task. Knowing that the other men will face the possibility of death, Erik recommends Hans for the job.

Alex Steiner

Alex Steiner is Rudy Steiner's father. He works as a tailor and owns his own clothing store in Molching. When Nazi officials want to take Rudy to a special officer's school due to his athletic and academic prowess, Alex refuses to let him go. Because of this, he is sent off to help with the war effort. Though he survives, his entire family is killed by the bombing of Himmel Street.

Kurt Steiner

Kurt Steiner is Rudy Steiner's older brother. When Rudy begins to have trouble with Frans Deutscher, Kurt manages to get Rudy transferred to a different Hitler Youth division.

Rudy Steiner

Rudy Steiner is Liesel's best friend, frequent companion, and occasional partner in thievery. He often looks out for Liesel and frequently attempts—unsuccessfully—to get her to kiss him. Rudy is terrorized by his Hitler Youth leader, Franz Deutscher; after switching Hitler Youth groups, however, he excels at both athletics and academics.

Nazi officials notice this and ask his parents to allow him to attend a special Nazi officer's school they are creating. Rudy's parents refuse to let him go. He dies with his mother and siblings when the bombs are dropped on Himmel Street.

Erik Vandenburg

Erik Vandenburg is Hans Hubermann's closest friend. The two served together during World War I. Vandenburg, a Jew, teaches Hans how to play the accordion and is responsible for Hans surviving when Vandenburg and everyone else in their unit are killed in combat: he saves Hans by recommending him for a noncombat project. Hans keeps Vandenburg's accordion and promises his wife that he will do whatever he can to repay the debt he owes to Vandenburg for saving his life.

Max Vandenburg

Max Vandenburg, the son of Erik Vandenburg, is a Jew who is taken in by Hans Hubermann. He lives for a time in the Hubermanns' basement and becomes close friends with Liesel. He makes Liesel two books of stories and sketches. Eventually, he leaves the Hubermanns' basement because he fears capture. Later, he is indeed captured, and Liesel sees him being marched through town on the way to a concentration camp. Max survives, and after the war he reunites with Liesel.

Reinhold Zucker

Reinhold Zucker is a fellow soldier in Hans's unit during World War II. When playing cards, he is a gloating winner and a sore loser. After Hans takes all of his cigarettes (used in place of money), Zucker gets angry and holds a grudge against him. Later, Zucker forces Hans to change seats with him on the transport truck as they head out to duty. The truck rolls over, and Zucker is the only one on board who is killed.

THEMES

Storytelling

Perhaps the most important theme found in *The Book Thief* is the power of stories. Most of the major events in the story revolve around this theme. Even Hitler's rise to power, it is suggested, is largely the result of the popularity of his autobiography, *Mein Kampf*. Later, the power of this book is used against the Nazi cause: Hans hides the key he sends to Max inside a copy of it, knowing that no one would suspect the sender (or receiver) of such a book to be engaging in suspicious activities. The book serves a final purpose when Max tears out its pages and paints over them to create his own stories.

For Liesel, her first book helps her hold on to the memory of her dead brother and absent mother. It is also the gateway for Liesel to forge a loving relationship with Hans, who teaches her how to read using the book. Stories later bind Liesel to Max, who creates his own homemade books as gifts to her since he has nothing else to offer. Ilsa Hermann is tied to Liesel by books as well: she spies the girl stealing one from the burning remains of the bonfire, and later invites her into her massive library. Their relationship is almost ended by written words—the letter Ilsa gives her for Rosa Hubermann, terminating her employment—and is also saved by them when Ilsa writes Liesel a letter of apology and gives her a dictionary.

Finally, stories save Liesel's life. Because she is in the basement, rereading her work on her own memoir, she is the only survivor on Himmel Street when the Allied bombs are dropped. It is this book that leads Death to remember and share Liesel's story with the reader.

The novel, however, also depicts certain limitations to the power of stories and the written word. For Hans, letters are insufficient to convey his thoughts and emotions while he is away as a soldier. Also, books are dependent upon one thing for their power: a reader. The books lining the walls of Ilsa Hermann's library serve no function—and indeed, the room itself appears cold and lifeless—until Liesel begins reading there. Liesel's own story is never read by another living soul and is tossed onto a pile of trash after the bombing. It is very nearly lost before Death spots it and saves it.

Dualism

Dualism is the presence of different—often opposing—forces or traits in a single thing or person. Duality is used throughout *The Book Thief* to emphasize both the wonderful and terrible possibilities of humankind.

This natural dualism is shown in nearly every character, including the most virtuous. Liesel herself is, as the title suggests, a thief; taken out of the context of her life, many of her actions would be considered immoral or worthy of punishment. She steals books, food, and even money from her foster mother, and she destroys one of Ilsa Hermann's books. Hans Hubermann, described as having eyes "made of kindness," strikes Liesel hard across the face when she makes a disparaging statement about Hitler in public. He later threatens her with awful consequences if she ever reveals the secret of Max Vandenburg. He does these things for her protection, and he does them reluctantly; however, this illustrates the potential within even the most virtuous people to hurt those they love.

TOPICS FOR FURTHER STUDY

- One of the most important and tragic events in *The Book Thief* is the nighttime air bombing of Himmel Street by Allied forces. Indeed, World War II was the first war to feature large-scale bombings of nonmilitary targets, also known as "strategic bombing." Research the topic of strategic bombing during World War II. Who engaged in it, for what reasons, and how were the targets chosen? What did this accomplish, and what were the consequences? In your opinion, was the practice justified by what it accomplished? Do you think the bombing of civilian targets is justified in other situations? Why or why not? In an oral report accompanied by a presentation with multimedia or visual support (such as graphs showing civilian casualty figures), summarize your findings and take a position on the issue of strategic bombing.

- A popular childhood chant states, "Sticks and stones may break my bones, but names will never hurt me." Victims of insults are often told that the offense is "just words." Under most circumstances in the United States, the accepted definition of assault is that it begins not when someone shouts abuse at another person, but when physical contact is made. The main message of *The Book Thief*, however, is rather opposite: that words are among the most powerful tools known to humankind. Do you think words hold the same power as physical action? Why or why not? Provide examples—from your personal experience or from historical research—to support your point in a reflective essay.

- The Hitler Youth organization was meant to indoctrinate young Germans in the ideas and beliefs of the Nazi Party. Enrolling in the Hitler Youth was made mandatory in 1939, though enforcement was often lax; many young people, as shown in *The Book Thief*, thought the organization was beneficial only as an athletic or social organization, and ignored or dismissed its ideological underpinnings. After the end of World War II, however, many members of the Hitler Youth were persecuted for their implied support of the Nazis. Watch the movie *Swing Kids* (1993), about young adults coming of age in Nazi Germany, paying close attention to the significance of characters' participation in Hitler Youth groups. Do you think it is fair to condemn young people who participated in the Hitler Youth as supporters of Nazism? What about adults who were drafted to fight for Nazi Germany? In your opinion, at what point is the statement "I was just doing what I was forced to do" not an acceptable reason for unethical action? Giving consideration to these questions and others, write an essay comparing the depictions of the Hitler Youth in *The Book Thief* and *Swing Kids*.

- Books, stories, and words play significant roles in the upkeep of morale and even in the survival of characters in *The Book Thief*. Read *Balzac and the Little Chinese Seamstress* (2000), a novel by Dai Sijie that is suitable for young adults, and consider the role played by literature in the lives of his protagonists during China's Cultural Revolution. Write an essay comparing and contrasting the influence of stories on the characters in Zusak's and Sijie's novels.

Rosa Hubermann is a clearer example of duality. She is brash, insulting, and speaks venomously of nearly everyone with whom she comes into contact—especially her husband, Hans. When Hans is conscripted to serve in the war, however, her true feelings about him are revealed: Liesel discovers her sitting on the edge of her bed, cradling his accordion—an instrument she previously seemed to despise—and silently praying for his safe return. Similarly, though she constantly refers to Liesel as "*Saumensch*," Liesel eventually realizes that boundless love exists just beneath the superficial insult.

Duality is perhaps most dramatically shown in Death's observations of humans. Seeing people's lives end day after day, often at the hands of other people, Death notes that he is "constantly overestimating and underestimating the human race." In his final conversation with Liesel, he states about humans, "I wanted to ask her how the same thing could be so ugly and so glorious, and its words and stories so damning and brilliant."

Fate

Through cause and effect as well as chance, characters in *The Book Thief* are sometimes depicted as deserving of their fates owing to their past actions. But on the whole, as told from Death's perspective, the book suggests that the universal fate of all human beings, an end to life, is simply unavoidable. As the narrator, Death takes great pains to delineate the interconnected nature of the actions and reactions of the characters. Although many events might be described as lucky or unlucky occurrences, their causes are nearly always revealed. Hans Hubermann, for example, manages to avoid death twice during military service—once during World War I, and again during World War

II. The first time, he is saved because his friend Erik Vandenburg recommends him for a noncombat assignment; the indebtedness he feels to Erik, who dies that day, eventually results in him taking in Erik's son Max, a Jew in hiding, twenty years later. This in turn causes dramatic changes in the lives of Liesel and Rosa as well. At the same time, Hans's friendship with Max results in an enduring sympathy for persecuted Jews, which ultimately leads to Max having to leave the Hubermann's basement for fear of discovery by Nazis suspicious of Hans. It also leads Hans back to military duty, pressed into service as a sort of punishment for his sympathizing with Jews.

Similarly, Hans escapes death a second time because he beats his fellow soldiers at cards—a game largely of chance. Even though he is gracious and offers some of his winnings back to the other players, his win angers another soldier, who later forces Hans to change seats with him on their transport truck. During that trip, the truck rolls over, and the other soldier—sitting where Hans would have sat—is the only casualty. In addition, Hans's generosity when winning at cards persuades his sergeant to recommend that he be able to return home to his family. This lucky turn of events results in Hans being present on Himmel Street when the Allied bombs are dropped, resulting in his death. However kindhearted all the people of Himmel Street may be, only Liesel is lucky enough to escape the fate of an untimely death in the bombing.

STYLE

Memoir

The Book Thief is written in the form of a memoir. A memoir is a personal record of events in the writer's own life. Hitler's *Mein Kampf*, mentioned often in the novel, is a memoir, as is the book that Liesel writes about her own experiences. In addition, *The Book Thief* itself often serves as a memoir for its narrator, Death; in addition to Death's own experiences with Liesel and the people in her life, there are also sections throughout the book labeled "Death's Diary" that relate brief glimpses of the narrator's other grim work during World War II.

Foreshadowing and Flash-Forwards

Foreshadowing, or the suggestion of what will happen later in the story, is used extensively in *The Book Thief*. The narrator frequently hints of what is to come later, as when he states in the prologue, "I saw the book thief three times." The author also uses flash-forwards, or glimpses at events that take place beyond the story's current time frame. For example, after revealing how many times he saw the book thief, the narrator goes on to provide detailed descriptions of each occasion—though two of those events will not take place until near the end of the book. Another example of foreshadowing occurs when Liesel convinces herself that Ilsa Hermann did not see her take a book from the bonfire. The narrator quickly offers, "The mayor's wife had seen her, all right. She was just waiting for the right moment." Similarly, when Viktor Chemmel threatens to make Rudy pay for spitting at him, the narrator informs the reader, "It took him approximately five months to turn his statement into a true one." The act of vengeance occurs twenty-five pages later.

The foreshadowing in *The Book Thief* often explicitly reveals the fates of the characters. The narrator tells the reader in no uncertain terms what will happen, as when he states about Reinhold Zucker shortly after introducing him, "He would die with his mouth open." The narrator also makes clear that Rudy Steiner will die, though the circumstances of his death are kept vague until the event occurs.

Stories within Stories

The Book Thief contains many stories within the main tale being told by the narrator. These include brief asides by the narrator that touch upon events not directly related to Liesel's story. In addition, the books Liesel reads are mostly fictional works, and the basic plot of each is described for the reader, often along with snippets of text from the book.

The clearest examples of stories within the

story, however, are the ones Max creates for Liesel. They are even presented in a different format than the rest of the book, in what is meant to represent Max's own handwritten and hand-drawn work.

The Rise of the Nazi Party and Hitler Youth

The Nazi Party, or the National Socialist German Workers' Party, rose to power in the wake of the economic turmoil Germany suffered after being defeated in World War I. Founded in 1918, the party focused on a platform of national unity and pride, coupled with the darker goals of driving Jews out of the country and expanding Germany's borders at the expense of neighboring countries. Adolf Hitler became a party member and quickly rose to the highest ranks due to his ambition and oratory skills. He attempted to seize control of the German government in 1923 but was unsuccessful and instead spent a little over one year in jail. During this time, he wrote *Mein Kampf* (My Struggle), a book that offered a positive and persuasive view of his actions and political beliefs.

As economic conditions worsened in the years that followed—in part due to the Great Depression, which had a drastic effect on the global economy— Hitler's promises of a prosperous Germany won over a large percentage of the population. By the early 1930s, the Nazi Party had won substantial power in the Reichstag, or German parliament, not by force but by election. Hitler, however—despite his popularity—was not elected. Instead, as the governing bodies of Germany fell into chaos, the president appointed Hitler chancellor of Germany. He quickly seized control of government and military offices, silencing his critics and any other social elements he considered undesirable.

The Hitler Youth was created in 1922, composed primarily of the children of Nazi Party members. Like the Nazi Party itself, the organization grew slowly but steadily until 1930, when membership expanded dramatically; between 1930 and 1934, Hitler Youth membership skyrocketed from 26,000 to over 3.5 million. As Michael H. Kater points out in *Hitler Youth*, "Many if not most of the youth cohort for the period of the 1920s and very early 1930s felt cheated out of what chances they had thought were theirs and increasingly looked to radical alternatives." The group was briefly banned in 1932 but was quickly reinstated in recognition of Hitler's influence and popularity.

The organization was meant to serve as premilitary training, and older members of the Hitler Youth almost inevitably went on to become Nazi soldiers fighting on the front lines or officers in charge of expanding Hitler Youth membership. Equivalent organizations for females and for younger children were also formed; these more closely resembled activity clubs than military groups, though they also provided the Nazi Party with an opportunity to indoctrinate youngsters with their beliefs. Although Hitler Youth began with voluntary membership, it was later required for all eligible German children.

As the German war effort faltered in the early 1940s, the Nazi Party began to call up younger and younger members of the Hitler Youth to active duty in the national militia. Members as young as fourteen were called upon to serve in antiaircraft units and were killed in the increased bombings within Germany's borders. With the defeat of Germany in 1945 by Allied forces, the Hitler Youth and its related organizations were quickly disbanded. Many German children who had been forced into compulsory Hitler Youth programs were often stigmatized later in life due to their involvement with organizations so closely associated with Nazism.

The Allied Bombing of German Cities

As Allied forces waged war against Germany and the other Axis powers during World War II, British (and later American) air forces began bombing raids on German-occupied areas of Europe that were not considered combat locations. The justification for these bombings was twofold: to begin with, the targets for these bombings were often strategic pieces of German industry or infrastructure, meaning that their destruction would weaken Germany's ability to continue supporting its troops with weaponry and other essentials; also, it was believed that destruction of some nonmilitary targets would serve to weaken the morale of

German citizens and erode support for Hitler and the Nazi Party.

Between the British Royal Air Force and the United States Air Force, over 1.5 million tons of bombs were dropped on Germany between 1939 and 1945. Munich, the large city near which Liesel and her foster family live in *The Book Thief*, was subjected to over seventy separate bombing attacks by air. One of the worst bombings, however, was reserved for the city of Dresden in February 1945. The city was obliterated in two days of nonstop attacks, as the bombs set off fires that raged uncontrolled in their wake. Conservative estimates of civilian casualties in Dresden—deaths of those not involved in combat in any way—exceed 20,000, and some believe that as many as 40,000 German citizens were killed.

In all, historians estimate that approximately 600,000 German civilians were killed by Allied bombings during the war—dwarfing the estimated loss of around 14,000 British citizens due to German air attacks. One in every nine German civilian casualties was a child. Because of these startling statistics, the practice of bombing in city areas has been a source of great controversy ever since.

CRITICAL OVERVIEW

When *The Book Thief* was published in 2005 as a book for children and young adults, it met with initial skepticism regarding its length (over five hundred pages) and its subject matter (a child living in Nazi Germany surrounded by death, as narrated by Death). However, reviews for the novel were overwhelmingly positive, which helped to propel the book to the status of best seller.

Most of the praise for the work centered on the resonant power of the story, though the author's skill with language was also complimented in many reviews. Francisca Goldsmith, in a review for *School Library Journal*, calls the book "an extraordinary narrative." Goldsmith observes that the author "not only creates a mesmerizing and original story but also writes with poetic syntax." Claire E. Gross, reviewing the novel for the *Horn Book* magazine, refers to it as a "deeply affecting tale." She remarks, "Exquisitely written and memorably populated, Zusak's poignant tribute to words, survival, and their curiously inevitable entwinement is a tour de force to be not just read but inhabited."

Michael Cart, in a brief recommendation from *Booklist*, expresses pleasant surprise over the novel's achievements: "Who would have thought that Death could be such an engaging—even sympathetic—narrator? And has there ever been a better celebration of the lifesaving and affirming power of books and the reading of them?" In a review for *School Libarary Journal*, Barbara Wysocki compliments the "richly evocative imagery and compelling characters" of the novel, while April Brannon, writing for the *Journal of Adolescent and Adult Literacy*, points out the "surreal and often stunning" imagery created by the author.

Some reviews of the book included brief cautions about the subject matter and its appropriateness for young readers. Brannon notes that the book "is set in the bleakest of circumstances but is a surprisingly hopeful story about the atrocities that occurred during the Nazi years in Germany." She suggests that the book "would work best with high school audiences." Goldsmith seems to agree, stating that the novel "deserves the attention of sophisticated teen and adult readers."

Lev Grossman, in a review for *Time*, recommends the book for "more ambitious younger readers." He specifically notes that the opening pages of the book are "rather challenging." Grossman further notes, "Zusak doesn't sugarcoat anything, but he makes his ostensibly gloomy subject bearable the same way Kurt Vonnegut did in *Slaughterhouse-Five*: with grim, darkly consoling humor." A reviewer in *Publishers Weekly* calls Zusak's novel "a challenging book in both length and subject, and best suited to sophisticated older readers." The reviewer also notes that despite the often dark subject matter, the author's "playfulness with language leavens the horror and makes the theme even more resonant." The reviewer does point out, however, that the narrator "has a bad habit of forecasting" upcoming events. Hazel Rochman, in her largely positive review for *Booklist*, concedes that the novel has "too much commentary at the outset, and too much switching from past to present time."

The Book Thief earned the top spot on the *New York Times* children's best-seller list and remained on the list for over five months. It has also been a number-one seller in Ireland, Taiwan, and Brazil. The book was named a Michael L. Printz Honor Book in 2007, and it earned the Kathleen Mitchell Award and the Teen Book Award from the Association of Jewish Libraries. Hailed as a phenomenal title for adults and younger readers alike, *The Book Thief* has continued to enjoy widespread popularity into the 2010s.

SOURCES

Blasingame, James, Cynthia Kiefer, David M. Pegram, Kyle Gillis, Bryan Gillis, April Brannon, and Megan Hoover, "Books for Adolescents," in *Journal of Adolescent & Adult Literacy*, Vol. 49, No. 8, May 2006, pp. 718–27.

Cart, Michael, "'Tis the Season," in *Booklist*, Vol. 103, Nos. 9–10, January 1, 2007, p. 74.

Davis, Richard G., *Bombing the European Axis Powers: A Historical Digest of the Combined Bomber Offensive, 1939–1945*, Air University Press, 2006.

Goldsmith, Francisca, Review of *The Book Thief*, in *School Library Journal*, Vol. 52, No. 3, March 2006, p. 234.

Gross, Claire E., Review of *The Book Thief*, in *Horn Book*, Vol. 82, No. 2, March–April 2006, pp. 199–200.

Grossman, Lev, "5 Great New Books: Dragons! Lip Gloss! Death! There's Life in Teen Books after Harry Potter," in *Time*, Vol. 167, No. 11, March 13, 2006, p. 63.

Harding, Luke, "Germany's Forgotten Victims," in *Guardian* (London, England), October 22, 2003, http://www.guardian.co.uk/world/2003/oct/22/world (accessed March 19, 2008).

Kater, Michael H., *Hitler Youth*, Harvard University

Press, 2004, p. 6.

Lamers, Richard, "Destroyed Youth: Growing Up in Nazi Germany," Goethe-Institut website, November 2007, http://www.goethe.de/ges/pok/dun/en2744598.htm (accessed March 18, 2008).

Maughan, Shannon, "It's a Wonderful (Sales) Life: The Staying Power of 'The Book Thief,'" in *Publishers Weekly*, Vol. 257, No. 34, August 30, 2010, p. 16.

Rempel, Gerhard, *Hitler's Children: The Hitler Youth and the SS*, University of North Carolina Press, 1989.

Review of *The Book Thief*, in *Publishers Weekly*, Vol. 253, No. 5, January 30, 2006, pp. 70–71.

Rochman, Hazel, Review of *The Book Thief*, in *Booklist*, Vol. 102, Nos. 9–10, January 1, 2006, p. 88.

Wysocki, Barbara, Review of *The Book Thief*, in *School Library Journal*, Vol. 53, No. 3, March 2007, p. 79.

Zusak, Markus, *The Book Thief*, Knopf, 2007.

FURTHER READING

Gottfried, Ted, *Children of the Slaughter: Young People of the Holocaust*, Twenty-First Century Books, 2001.

> This compact volume discusses both the young Jewish victims of the Holocaust and the German young people manipulated through the Hitler Youth. With text presented in capsule format, the book is especially readable for young adults.

Hitler, Adolf, *Mein Kampf*, translated by Ralph Manheim, Educa Books, 2006.

> This book, part autobiography and part political diatribe, reveals the thoughts, motivations, and goals of one of the world's most destructive leaders. Written before his rise to prominence and after his first failed attempt to take over the government, *Mein Kampf* contains the same fervent nationalism, brutality, and racial hatred that later marked the era of Nazi rule. It provides important insight for those interested in understanding the tragic roots of World War II and the Holocaust.

Wall, Donald D., *Nazi Germany and World War II*,

2nd ed., Thomson/Wadsworth, 2003.

> Historian Donald D. Wall provides a comprehensive overview of Germany before and during World War II. The book covers the conditions that brought about the rise of Hitler and the Nazi Party, the German perspective on Hitler, and how such a massive atrocity as the Holocaust could have happened at all.

Wiesel, Elie, *Night*, Hill & Wang, 2006.

> This haunting memoir chronicles the author's experiences as a young man in concentration camps at Dachau and Buchenwald. Wiesel received a Nobel Peace Prize in 1986, primarily for the impact of this work, which was first published in Yiddish in the mid-1950s and was translated into English in 1960.

SUGGESTED SEARCH TERMS

Markus Zusak AND The Book Thief

The Book Thief AND Holocaust

Holocaust AND young adult literature

Holocaust AND children's literature

The Book Thief AND death

Nazi Party AND Hitler Youth

Nazi Party AND literature

Markus Zusak AND interview

Printed in June 2019
by Rotomail Italia S.p.A., Vignate (MI) - Italy